I0518518

Fatherless Children

an elegy for my father

poetry by

Michael D. Grover

ROADSIDE PRESS

Editor: Michele McDannold

Roadside Press
Colchester, Illinois

Fatherless Children
(An Elegy For My Father)

-1-

In the Akash of the evening
The craft of writing returns to me
Like something's been building
It has to go somewhere
It has to be born like a bomb
In a blast of energy
I have no idea where this Poem's gonna go
But it's about time to get rid of all that expectation
All I know is that at the end of this Poem
I will not know my father
I will never know my father
Same way he never knew his father
So here we are all just fatherless children of america
So we had best be resilient
We had best be ready for a shitstorm
Because there's always one around the corner
Just like Budha said
A real life realm of suffering
Akash settles over like a fine mist
Sun sets the sky on fire in the distance

-2-

We, the fatherless children of america
So badly in need of feminine balance
We might be children of the World
Just can't see it, limited conditioning
Far away from a universal mind
We are so busy running from the past

We run further from what we are
I understand how you got lost
I forgive you father
We all take the conditioning
We all drink the Floride
We all accept the truth
Rather than believing the things we really see
Those voices, higher guidance, who would believe any of this shit
I've only come so far because I've had lots of help
I can see believing the conning preacher
Seeking something to fill this whole inside
Forgive us fatherless children we don't ourselves
Did you ever wake up and not recognize yourself
Same as no one ever recognizes
We are real life humans beings out here
Not pawns in some twisted ego game
We're only treated like subhuman species
Less than human

-3-
A pack of road dogs
Running the country for scraps of work
Damn your family values comedy
There is no family in there
Just perfectly placed laugh tracks
To mark every tragedy, so much laughing

I visited my father in Boston, New Jersey, and New York City
He would fly me out for the Summer
Rolling around to where the work was
I once drove from LA to Everette, Washington
He had tried a fresh start, new marriage, same him

All of his union brothers would rave about what a "Good
brother" he was
Maybe he just never figured how to be a father
He never had anyone to show him
How could we blame him
We are the fatherless rage of a fatherless age
Our righteous punk rock rage
Nowhere to direct it
So we just accept it

-4-
Life goes on they say
Every time someone dies
I guess that's really all there is to say
These days I feel so unmotivated
The vultures took everything
Not so liberal or compassionate
But you know the deal
Depends on who's deal your buying
And they're all full of lies
You knew what the deal was

-5-
You were the one that gave me the spark
That old beat up Beat Reader
Still sitting on my bookshelf
That spark I've drug all over the country with me
Maybe that was you saying goodbye to your dreams
As I said hello, who knew I would take it so far
But what was I supposed to do
You gave me the red manifesto
I left that with an anarchist in Philly

She said she'd never read it
Or Emma Goldman, and what kind of anarchist had never read
Goldman
Was I so wrong to follow it
I guess it's all pointless now
There is no one left to have this discussion with
Other than myself

-6-
The only advice my father ever gave me as a writer
Don't give it all away for free

-7-
We the fatherless children of america
Blowing around like tumbleweeds through the American dream
Couldn't afford to pay attention
Much less know what a father is
                    what a man is
So we always have something to prove
Always acting from the ego
Just as we were always taught
Can't talk about stuff like feelings
No real shit
Forgive us for never seeing
That it was all connected

-8-
I've been working on my ego a lot lately
I wonder if you ever worked on yours
I take it you didn't since you were too proud to call back
After that last time you hung up on me
I wanted this to end different

Like that wasn't out last conversation
Technically it wasn't
I wanted to have a conversation with you
There is so much left to discuss
Besides it gets lonely here
Just me every minute, every day
Healing trauma
Healing cancer
Healing …

-9-
I don't have regrets
I could not have done this different
It was in your hands
That is the way it's gonna be
This is the way america has always been
Like Buddha's realm of suffering
I have suffered plenty
I am in need of rest & purification
So I may stay close to myself
Something everyone has pushed me from all my life
I really have so much work to do

-10-
Father, I've never hated Poetry before
But I'm learning
Too many years
Poetry not being a valid profession
I'm beginning to see how it's ruined my life
No one really talks to me anymore, they just die
There is nothing left to work on after that
All my life feeling like a stranger in a strange land

In this strange World, with your strange Poems
Men too gentle to live with wolves
All that was ever to say is they got eaten
Wolves do play with their food
Somehow I've lasted this long
You always did say "You've gotta be tough to be stupid"
Of course you were speaking directly to me
Yet here I am writing your elegy
I've seen too much suffering, written too many elegies
But I know it's my obligation
 carry on with life

-11-
At the local barber shop a ten-year-old kid
Savors the latest edition of Shooters Digest
As big brother sits in the chair
Looking at the ads he tells his mother
That he wants that one, that one, and that one
His father comes up rattling off all the letters and numbers

Father you used to take us to the Smokey Mountains every year
You would set up your empty beer cans, and shoot your Glock at
them
You would make me shoot, the sound bothered me, and I jerked
the gun
I guess I failed in that right of passage, but my sister shot the gun
well
And you would be proud of one of us

-12-
Is the World so cruel
Trying to manifest something better

All I get is suffering
What I'm learning is self-mastery
How not to react to any situation
I believe that is the best way
It was you that always taught me
Wish in one hand shit in the other
See which one fills up first

-13-
I've learned how to let go
The art of surrender
That way you don't have to be
Fighting against yourself all the time
Inertia in motion
I took some real time to quiet my mind
Now I know myself better
Funny thing is that I found myself there
I know just what I am

I wonder if you ever got to know yourself
If you ever learned to put yourself aside
That ego of so many masks
                    so many voices in the head
Did you ever figure out what is real

-14-
Everything they ever taught us was a lie
What you taught me
What you were taught
All of the churches
All of the bullshit
All of the shit they puke on you in his-story lower class

Everything beyond that
All of that ego & pride
You think that's you talkin'

-15-
The winners always love america
You'll hear them singing its greatness
They always stand for the anthem
Vultures leading the poor to grow more
& we all know how the story goes
We fatherless children of america are tired
We've seen too much destruction & the big money behind it
I see kindness in the street raped, & beaten
I'm not sure we should be around anymore

-16-
You were the one that handed me the fire
                                    the desire
Grinding against the system, so full of punk rock angst
                                so full of angst
                                so empty
Like a fatherless child of america
We don't know what the answers are
We don't know anything
We don't know what's a lie, and what the truth is
Rage on fatherless children, rage on
Even when you don't know what you're raging for, just rage

-17-
What's left but to live
We could all die tomorrow
So I've learned the hard way

Something else I've learned
Is that I'm pretty damned hard to kill
It's the coming back that's the hard part

-18-
Stormy evening,
Cold front coming through
Mid-March
Could be the last one of the year
New portals, new possibilities, new years
Always changing on the last one
Impermanence everywhere of everything

-19-
Life too much thinkin', contemplating
Whatever happens to a dream deferred
Countin' lost hours of the best years of our lives
Buildin' other people's dreams

-20-
The common voice is never heard
We don't own newspapers, tv stations, radio stations,
Book publishers, play station, or any station
We just consume what they feed us
Cancer today, maybe tomorrow a pandemic
We buy it, all the fear that comes with it
Selling our souls cheap
Hustling ourselves to the highest bidder
This america that teaches that slavery was abolished
Work will set you free
Nothing's free anymore
Not even freedom, they will be quick to tell you

We the fatherless children of america
We just want the freedom that was ascribed to us
Freedom to write and not starve
How is that for a start

-21-
Some other Poet passed on
I don't have the words or energy anymore
He once wrote a solid eulogy for Kaufman
Another page of history dies unheard
I can't hear anything anymore
Another witness & the World looks darker
Here it's cloudy & windy, crazy Jazz plays
Wind makes the leaves whisper,
        makes the trees dance
It's chaotic this life
When you can only control your own actions
When you can't control outside forces
Self-mastery is the key
To not react to anything
To just sit back and enjoy the ride
It's all they will let us do

-22-
Church is every day
Under the avocado tree
Six-thirty Sabbath
Come ready to bleed
It's not just the mosquitos
That draw blood around here
It's the words in you're head being born
It's a storm of wild spontaneous Jazz

Right now the Reverend Mingus has the stage
Crashing into crescendo
This Poem goes on,
Because that's what I do

-23-
With death always lingering
Just outside the realm of sight
Always wondering who's next
Who wins this unlucky lottery
It keeps you on your toes
Impermanence of everything
It's not just you
Your friends, your parents, your dog
It's a whole shitshow
That you don't want to go through
Enjoy this human existence gone so wrong
There were a lot of good times in there
None of them matter
There was plenty of suffering
That didn't matter
Most people won't read this until after I'm dead
And that doesn't matter
That's the Poets contract
It's a shitty deal
And that doesn't matter
All that matters is now, here, at this very second
I am the writer. Sitting under the avocado tree
Smoking a bowl, drinking an iced coffee
Listening to some Charles Earland funky assed Jazz
Sun sets on another birthday
                    another year

And you the reader, whereever you may be
You are right here in this experience that we just shared
And maybe by now you're figuring out this Poem is getting weird
And you're probably right about that
But that shared experience between writer and reader is all that
matters
Living in the shadow of artists who have died for this craft
It can be a heavy load
It can make you bitter, this bitch we call Poetry
But I've been taking the time to get to know it again
In my own special way

-24-
Old age is a cruel joke
Just watching your friends die
Going through the same cycles
Never evolving as a species
Stuck in a trap
Did you ever feel just like a hamster in a wheel
Did you ever feel your body fall apart
Did you ever remember when you thought you were invincible
Did you feel more vulnerable like prey in the end

-25-
Who would write about history
If the Poets weren't there to do it
Who indeed, not me, been too busy struglin'
Trying to get a moments rest
But the words won't write themselves,
Or type themselves up
Believe me I've tried
There's a storm blowing over

It's mostly broken up
Dark trees dancing in a dark sky
Freddy Hubbard bringing it all home

-26-
Strange days we are walking through
Energies like I've never felt before
Something dark, twisted, and sinister
I can't see it, but I can feel it
Lingering just beneath the surface
Of what we call reality
Something feeding on our negative energy
I felt something in the mist this morning
When I went out to walk the dogs
Something telling me to stay home

-27-
Here we practice alchemy
We transmute fear to positive energy
Sun setting on another day
Nothing much got done
But everything got checked off the list
Nothing left to do but sit back and enjoy life

-28-
Sun sets into the tree
Becomes a sphere of light between branches
Neighbors flag sags sadly
Some kind of metaphor for an american dream

-29-
I feel a heaviness today

Like a weight
That pulls back down
When I try to get up
I just go easy on days like this
I know you had cancer in the end
I wonder if it ever humbled you
It has a way of doing that

-30-
This is an elegy for the World you knew
It doesn't exist anymore
Impermanence surging forward
Just go with the flow
Like a movie in your head
Jazz in your head the soundtrack
A wild wind blowing in the trees like Jazz

-31-
This is a conjuring
Conjuring words
Always has been
Always will be
That rush of words
Stream of conscience
In my head
As the birds chirp
As the Jazz plays
As music plays from another back yard
We're all just back together
As the dogs play
As the sun sets in my eyes

-32-
Everyone has personal struggles
Passing through struggle after struggle
It's hard to tell yourself to stop struggling
The struggle is our life
Our very existence is struggle
We need it to be
We are nothing without the struggle
We will struggle against anything
Did you ever grow tired of struggling

-33-
Too close to go back
I keep on walkin'
Don't know where I'm goin'
Or how I will get there
I just keep walking forward
Knowing that this is the path
It keeps getting clearer
I don't think it's time to quit yet
I don't see the point in going on
Maybe there really was a point to all of this

-34-
History spiraling downward, spiraling
As the foundation of lies they have taught us all
Falls on its head
People clinging like abused and traumatized children
It turns out we're all responsible for anything and everything
And I'm still paying it off
Things they never taught us like meditation
It's almost like they never wanted us to come out of this

All I can do anymore is move forward
There was a solar eclipse today
I saw it from here with my safety glasses
I saw it from Houston, Texas, Arkansas, and Illinois
Dragging it's darkness across america, and youtube
Maybe it's all a bad joke
Maybe it's all too real

-35-
At the end of suffering
Will there really be a need for Poetry
Or just a blissful silence, nothing comes
All of this calm, what a silly World to write of

-36-
I see no remains of my father
No phone call
No funeral
It's like he never died
Because he was never there
Like memory is just a movie
Move along and return to your lives
If you hang on, you can't hang around here
The next show will be starting soon

-37-
Look at me, you can see what it has done
Following Poetry into decades of madness
Following Poetry into being an outcast
Following Poetry into the role of black sheep
Surely not a lot redeemable
Maybe in another universe where people care about literature
Maybe only after we die

-38-

I watch another sunset
Big ball of light setting
Through the leaves of a tree
The other day the sun was eclipsed
It was still a big ball of light
Until you put on the special glasses
You could see a slither of the ball was missing
Father, there is something missing
I know the answers are never coming
I am not waiting for anything
Recovery from death is hard
Brain doesn't always work the way you want it to
I have nothing to do but wait here
I know there is nothing coming

-39-

War erupts somewhere
Always evil men doing dark, ritualistic things
Sacrificing lives for some dark energy
Sacrificing lives but profits are up
War always our greatest fear
Somewhere two-thousand pound bombs are dropping
For no reason, just extinction
We watch from far away, run away
Fear, the greatest power they could ever hold over us
It holds us like abused children
Negative emotions to feed the elite, and they are very hungry
The darkness at the soul of america
War master, puppet master
We just move on and try to forget
That it's all impermanent

-40-
Cosmic Jazz rising from the backyard
Along with puffs of marijuana
Dogs prowling the huge backyard like hunters
Words finally appear on the page
Sun sets behind the tree on another day

-41-
We the fatherless children of america
Suffering is our only birthright
No rights in the eyes of corporate law
Just a slave to the system
Is god someone you can hang out with
Or is he like the president
Or some other important rich person
Making important decisions I could never comprehend
Every day I walk, I feel a step closer to the real God
I've got a list of complaints and questions
About billionaire christian dictators begging for money on
youtube
Says he's got a new version of the bible, only a hundred bucks,
what a bargain

-42-
(For William Carlos Williams)
The sound of leaves is silence
Under the avocado tree as the leaves blow
Trane blows saxophone, drum roll supreme please
Car horns, & dog tails, neighbor's flag perpetually at half-mast
Is there any symbolism to that

-43-
Out in the void
Endless field, nothing but space
Nothing but darkness to linger inside
I wonder if you ever saw it
Maybe passed through on the way out
I've seen too much of it
Stuck in my own mind
I had to shake my way out of there
I didn't think I ever would
There is not a lot of hope for anything there
I came out of it far different than I went in

-44-
By fear we fall
Fear so ingrained in us
Will we ever rise above
Fear is the enemy
Love is the cure
Fear less, love more
I hope you went in light and peace
Away from the darkness in this World
Away from the darkness in your head
I hope you found light in the end

-45-
Earth our carcass
Flies are gathering
Vultures are circling
Man keeps pressing forward

Like it wasn't the end of days
Like it was just another day
I miss the World as it used to be
Something changed in my sleep
I must've slept for years

-46-
Mixing the pure madness of an Earland jam
To the Poetic madness as the sun is setting
Dogs play, another day of ordinary life ends
We'll see what the night brings

-47-
Father we have failed
At the simple task of loving each other
I guess it's too fucking easy to hate
Hate is all they ever gave us
Hate is all we've ever known
I am trying things a different way
I am living with love & compassion
And I'll do it openly
I'm sure people won't recognize me
They might call me anti-american
After president trump wins the election
I must be an alien
& maybe I am

-48-
Beauty is wasted
Not appreciated here
Artists as much as you want to make this World beautiful
You can paint over it,

try to paint a new one
Good luck with that
It will never seem to manifest
Not the way you envisioned it
We all fall in the end
One way or the other
Me I'm still standing here
They keep me around as long as my insurance is good

-49-
Maybe I think about you more dead
Sitting under this tree writing more to you
Maybe I could have been a better son
Maybe I could have been something respectable
Not a low down street Poet
Maybe we would have talked more,
Or talked kindly to each other
Maybe you would not have hung up
That last time I called
We could never change anything now
I've been writing to you every day for two months now
& I can't see myself stopping anytime soon

-50-
You never met Docker
He was a good loyal Jack Russel
He helped me get through a lot of shit
He spent years right beside me
When I couldn't get out of the recliner
We grew old and fat together
He died a month before you did
Now I have a Corgi

He fills me with joy every day
Maybe someday I won't think of you
Maybe someday I will end this Poem
Not today

-51-
Do you still have to struggle
Just to fucking exist out there
Because I'm sick of struggling
That steady downhill climb
I guess that's life, still climbing to survive
It's never fucking easy street
Everyday I beat myself down
Just to get up and do it the next day
By the magic of weed & crystals, I have risen

-52-
The neighbors flag flaps sadly in the wind
Maybe it's a message, maybe it's just the wind
It's kind of sad
With the tv talkin' about the inconvenience of all these protests
With all this war goin' on

-53-
I have suffered for my art, what artist hasn't
Poetry and I aren't really on speaking terms
Yet, here I sit, it's a complicated relationship
Yet here it is, not because I want to, because I have to

-54-
Langston said "Death is a drum
Telling life to come, come, come"

It does wake you up
I don't know where I've been
I know I've seen too much shit
Forgive me

-55-
Students tear gassed at an anti-war protest
An hour away from here in Tampa
Because the governor said the protest was too peaceful
So he shot tear gas at it
He signed concealed carry laws
He doesn't want peaceful anything

-56-
Sometimes I read a Poem so real
That I just stop and say
That's some fucked up shit
It's all life anyway
It's only real if you believe it

-57-
I'm inspired by the protesters of the war
It tells me it's not all doom & gloom out there
But now the cops have ladders
Now the real doom & gloom begins
It could be worse, you could be rotting away with cancer
But I've been working on alchemy & energy
I'm still learning

-58-
The World needs open communication
The problem is most people don't give a fuck about you

This leads to isolation, mid-life crisis, dark night of the soul type shit
Some people call it Kundalini, a spiritual awakening
Slowly putting the World back together
With all the lies we've been told
With all the things they don't want us to know
I am learning the World looks awful different
Given this new information
Everything feels awful different from what I used to know
Could be a mind tired from decades of constant stress
I can't say what's wrong with me
I know it's something that I'm working on
I keep cheating death a little more
I've been writing on this for a couple of months now
It doesn't seem to be going anywhere

-59-
Fight or flight when trauma comes
Too hard, too fast
You might get stuck in that mindset
Nervous all the time
Don't know why
Nothing on the horizon
There's always something

-60-
I've become less bitter
Not so worried about things I can't control
Like the government, always trying to control
Poets, thinkers, we've always been out of control
They might even kill us, they often do
They still can never stop us

-61-
They have hidden the truth from us
The most simple truth
Truth of non-duality
All that we do in that rat maze
Is feed them our energy
I understand you never knew
I understand the jungle is all about survival
Fight or flight that feeling
Of anxiety all the time
& all of the voices in your head
You've gotta figure out the right ones to listen to

-62-
Blind visionaries looking into the future
The dead walk the lines of the mind
The mind is like no place I've ever seen
I'm pretty sure the airplanes are watching
They must be bored

-63-
The Poetry messiah wants you to know
There is no Poetry messiah like him
I still don't understand the need for a messiah
He doesn't like to be disrespected
So you'd best pay close attention
All of his young recruits or anyone stupid enough to listen
He gives them lame advice for lame Poetry
You can't say too much, get too deep
People will have no idea what you're talking about

-64-
Everyday I meditate, and use positive affirmations
Like I'm trying to reprogram my mind
Maybe that's what I'm doing
Trying to fix what's broken
I just sit there, & do it instinctively
I never know why I do it
But I keep getting better
Still trying to fix what's broken
I guess we never stop doing that

-65-
We are all haunted houses
Walking around in flesh & bone
We all need exorcisms
But know nothing of energy, purification, or light
We know nothing of expansion, meditation, or transformation
We know nothing of his-story because we keep picking at those
scabs
We don't know alchemy, revolution, love
We the fatherless children of america should take the time to
know ourselves

-66-
A haunted house in flesh & bone
Sittin' in a chair in the backyard
The dog is running under the chair
Wind blowing, like Trane blowing
Under the watchful eye
Of a dragonfly sitting on a branch
A plane is circling
Big brother may be watching

Setting sun gets in my eyes
I'm tired, and I don't know why
I'm tired of the dogs barking at the neighbors
I'm tired of that plane circling

-67-
A story will be told in the end
Will you write your own story
Or follow someone else's plot
Go with the flow
As life rolls over you
Sacrificing the best hours of our lives
To corporate gods
Slaves sold in the town square
To the highest bidder

-68-
Father, you and I are forever strangers
Either of us will know the things we survived
I know that you survived quite a bit
I know that I have survived everything so far
Everybody survives everything they do
Trauma starts young reverberates through life

-69-
There is a blur in the sky
Where the sun's supposed to be
Days go by heavy like Florida humidity
In the morning air when I walk the dogs

-70-
Maybe the demons were always in our heads

Enough to fill the underworld a thousand times
The lizard in our brain driving us insane
The mind can be a whole World rarely explored
Who knows what is real, & what's projected anymore
Who knows if what they taught us is even true
There's a hole in the sky where the sun goes
Today was Buddha's Birthday, so I did an invocation
I felt his warmth in my heart
Strange days

-71-
Life does not slow down
There is no time out
It comes at you
Shattering that illusion that you had of control
Like there is any control
That is just another illusion
As if there could be a permanent pattern

-72-
I have way too much time on my hands
I am finding a link between Poets & mystics
How some Poets were mystics
Few knew success in their lifetime
Plath saw the insides of an oven
I heard today that Poets are Shaman
We walk into the underwold
Come out with a head full of words
What good is a Shaman with no tribe

-73-
Maybe none of it was real

It was all a simulation
It was all a reflection
It was all just our greatest fears
Memories that weren't really real
What are you supposed to do
When you wake up, and don't recognize yourself
You were becoming something totally different
All the while something just outside of the picture
It knows what you fear, it becomes fear
I know fear, been tryin' to stand up to it all my life
I've been diving into the underworld,
And coming out with a head full of words
Picking up a stream of conscious
I'm not afraid of it, it's a natural state to me
A perfect state of balance

-74-
Maybe I'm just looking for a reason
A reason to continue this forward motion
Tesla's self-propelled robot
The motion of recovery too slow
I tore down everything I thought I knew
Shedding it all like dead weight
                    like snake skin
All I know is daily practice, ritual
I have rebuilt myself out of instinct alone
I might even pass as human

-75-
That old Beat Reader that you left me
Serves as inspiration today with Mingus
That was the first place I ever read Howl

It's kept me company on many lonely night
Now it sits there next to Thoth
Ready to inspire future Poems

-76-
I am a man from a different time
Sittin' here watching times change
Just tryin' to remain the same
Everything a cycle
I have unlearned everything I knew
Now I only believe what I can see, or feel
I need to learn it all again
I remember when we sent submissions through snail mail
Months later the hand-printed zine would arrive in the mail
It was a lot of waiting, but it felt like something, it was real

-77-
Now things get harder
I had a scan yesterday
First scan I'd had in a year
I saw the doctor this morning to confirm
That everything is just the same
This makes no sense to me
It seemed like it was shrinking for a minute
Every time I think I know everything
It turns out I know nothing

-78-
Identity is everywhere
Images, stereotypes
People wearing bodies like identities
Trying to cover up the scars

-79-
I turn and forget
Everything fucked up about the World
I try to remember
Good times between the struggle
Or the peaceful times
Where there was nothing at all

-80-
The governor took the word extinction
Out of the state's vocabulary
Now when you say it people just give you a stupid stare
Like they don't know what you're trying to say
It's isolating being american
There's a lack of hope

-81-
Donald Trump a convicted felon
Still running for president
This must be some kind of simulation
Prison disguised as a free World
Fear is our only prison
We bury ourselves in it
So far away from ourselves
When we find ourselves it's too late

-82-
At what point did I truly lose my father
Was it that ten year old boy in the mountains of North Carolina
That was too big of a pussy to fire a gun
Well I'm proud to say that was the last time

Maybe that time you had to drive up to Philly
To get me out of a jam

Maybe it was that last Christmas
I couldn't make the family dinner
Because I couldn't move
Dark night of the soul type shit
I brought myself back from the dead, literally
I'm still somewhere in the middle
You always did say, "Progress is a slow process."
I am still trying to process what is haunting me
I am still trying to process what is happening
I keep on learning how little I really know
I know February 13th, the day I didn't know you died
I know I did not lose you on that day
No one bothered to tell me, so it never happened
Maybe those were your final wishes
I guess I'll never know
I figured out a while ago
That I don't need to know everything

-83-
I was raised by a kind father
Who saw my interest in writing
And tried to teach me Poetry
Never telling me it was gonna fuck up my life
Following it around, in and out of the underworld
Literally I mean
A true Shaman's journey
There was a Poet that said Poets were Shaman
I always held burying his ex-wife's unpublished Poems against
him
Think of the buried treasure

-84-
Writing in the rain
Dog running around
Trying to run between the drops

-85-
I am building myself back
And tearing myself down at the same time
I would never expect a person to learn from their mistakes
Just keep repeating the same cycles like an endless loop
Where has hope gone
Has anyone seen it around
It brightened the place up when it was around
I know they can't kill it

-86-
Father I have been thinking too much lately
Left alone with too many thoughts
Trying to transmute pain into love
A modern day alchemist
There is too much pain in this World
As I feel the pain inside of me
Imagine the pain of everyone
There is too much pain, and not enough love

-87-
It's been a long strange trip
Through this realm of suffering
Maybe you saw a different realm
While you were around
Maybe you saw a realm
That had an ounce of hope somewhere

Like the hope of the anti-war protests
As they are met with war of tear gas and rubber bullets
They crush hope here
History is just a cycle

-88-
They cannot kill our ghosts
We were already dead or dying
We've already done it so many times
What a time to be alive
To see a new beginning
To feel the shift of consciousness
Maybe there is a point to it at some point

-89-
I have stood face to face with riot police
With other Poets by my side
Funny thing about it, it was always peaceful
Until the cops showed up
In two-thousand your mother called me
My picture was on the front page of the Washington Post
Protesting the DNC in LA
She said she hoped I was okay

-90-
Most of the Poets in the books I own are dead
Some of them are still alive
Most Poets act like they don't know me

-91-
They told us death had honor
War heroes with medals

Death would be better
If we had money
Then people would suck up to us
Talk about how successful we were
There never was an american dream
For people like us
We just keep us building other people's dreams
What does it mean
This life, and death
What were we meant to learn
If anything at all
Just to sit in the backyard to write about this shit
Wind blowing raindrops out of the trees

-92-
The masks that we wear
Hiding us away in shame
Build them as high, & deep as we want
We build them, & hide
Then one day we wake up, and it's not there
Then you really start to know yourself
You build yourself back
Not the old self anymore
Bigger than self, part of the whole
I can't remember what I used to be
I needed to drop a lot of dead weight

-93-
Wars haunt our his-story
Echoing today, destroying
Screaming "Fear is control!"
In a crowded theater
Will they maintain control tomorrow

-94-
He called him a martyr
The billionaire ex/future president
He looked at the camera with a serious face
"I do it for my country."
The bullshit gets thick around here
So thick people can't see through it
That man would only be a martyr
In revisionist history
Which sounds about right for america
That feeds revisionist history to its young

-95-
After the rain
The air gets purified
Heaviness that we know as humidity
Gets lifted & the air feels lighter

-96-
It's father's day
I am writing a eulogy for my father
I don't know how long it is
I'm way behind on the typing
All that I know is that it's way too fucking long
I don't know how long this Poem intends to be
I'm just along for the ride

-97-
Poets we were born cursed
Cursed to live in our own hell
That we built all by ourselves

It's better than going into a hostile land
Where you really can't trust anyone
To be woke in Florida, that's a real curse
To see what these poor fuckers
Can't see coming right at them
Supreme court justices can't be corrupt
It was just a little trip to Bohemian Grove
First class all the way, what could go wrong

-98-
Everything just flat dead
Total lack of joy
Gray clouds blow over
Tomorrow maybe sun
We just don't know until it comes

-99-
Our sins are stubborn, like endless wars
Corporate advertiser suborn
Is there a way we can pay collectively
Because I've given more than my share
I'm still paying
I will always be paying

-100-
Metamorphosis, transmutation, transformation
Changing into something
Better than you used to be
Changing for the better
Leaving the old dead skin behind
Feel yourself rebuilding
Look back, see what you have created

Burn it all down, shed it like old skin
Unlearn everything you know, break the foundation
Becoming something you could never comprehend
The most authentic version of yourself

-101-
Long division, cracking, dividing
Ego & the need for importance
So desperate to change the World

-102-
We have no idea what love is
So all we ever do is hate
Nothing left to do
But grow better than we were
But we grow bitter & die from cancer
From the anger stored up inside
I can tell you, it's a bad way to go

-103-
The dog is barking and I don't know why
Doesn't he know I'm trying to write a Poem over here
There is magic in the air
The air doesn't feel so heavy

-104-
Today a storm got in the way
Of my daily writing ritual
So I waited for it to stop
So the air may be clear and free
Of the heaviness of the day, purified

-105-
I typed a little piece of this Poem up today
When I left off I was a month behind
I have a lot of typing to do
Maybe someday I'll catch up with myself

-106-
Masters of warfare and welfare
The american dream is an illusion
It always was
Work will set you free
Cheap death camp slogan
I don't know what to make of the modern World
It's the same as it ever was in the end
Masters and slave, but the slaves seem more willing
As factory machines eat grown humans whole
People in the street fighting for change
Tear gas and rubber bullet showers
Not a lot has changed

-107-
Tonight two white men will debate
To be the president of the stupid
I have no horse in the race
Only bad or mediocre choices
Only to be effected by decisions they make
Turning a blind eye to the darkness gnawing at our souls
As people die, and these men lie
The american dream is just that
As phony as a slick marketing campaign

-108-
The president lost his place in the great debate
Fell on his face
How many years must we suffer
Under christian nationalist fascism
They keep taking more
And we give willingly

-109-
Material World, always cluttered with things
Things that clutter your mind, create reality
To unplug, after being plugged in for so long
After being a slave for so long

-110-
Sometimes it's too easy
To get lost in my own head
Energy not flowing through my body
Sometimes it's too easy to get lost

-111-
Sweet & pretty evening
Everything just seems to flow
Like this Poem flows
Like Jazz flows
Like the evening flows

-112-
What is freedom
Did you ever find it
Were you ever free from your mind
What really is free

Were we born in captivity
Given a number at birth
Never knew freedom in our lives
But that time we went to the Marlins game
You couldn't stand for the national anthem
In a wheelchair, two broken legs
Looking over at me in disappointment

-113-
Did you ever feel free
Maybe at the end of the line
When you realize this material World
Isn't anything to worry about
Reality is subjective
One thing they never wanted us to know
Freedom is on the inside

-114-
Happy birthday america
Outside there is music, fireworks, cookouts
The neighborhood celebrates
It's gonna be a long night
The dogs won't sleep

-115-
I keep raising my vibration
Hopefully to the point that no disease can exist
That is hard to maintain

-116-
Moldavite on transformation
Like pouring gas on a fire

Let it burn slow
Like a Summer of climate change
So let's make it hotter
Let's get out of this limbo
I've been here too long
I just wanted motion

-117-
I went to my first protest with you
I was an apprentice for the union
A couple of other apprentices and I
Drove to Washington DC
To march at Solidarity Day
The union flew you there
So you met up with us
On the way back I learned to drive a stick shift
I haven't done it since

-118-
Years pass like oppression
Slow and hard
Suspended animation
Time doesn't matter when you're in the void
Getting out is a slow crawl
I feel almost human at this point
There is part of me that doubts that
There is part of me that tells me we don't get out
Maybe that's just fear talking

-119-
I almost feel alive again
Here in the backyard

Jazz is playin'
Poem is flowin'
Bird on it's perch chirpin'
Everything flowin' alive

-120-
Division & power
Rich gettin' richer
Negativity thicker than Florida humidity
I woke up and faced myself today
I have many things to work on
Many things I've changed so far
Things I've left behind

-121-
The material World is a lie
Where does the truth lie
What's the alternative
To fade away into nothing
Like a stranger in a strange land
Outside the realm of reality
I've been exploring my mind
Meditating everyday
I'm not finding a lot
But infinite space

-122-
This is not my country
Darkness manifested
Fear of god or any fear
Fear is the mindkiller
Bullet vending machines

Iron dome over the country
To block out higher intelligence

-123-
This is not my america
False flag assassination
For higher election points
People be damned
Actors gracefully dodge bullets like the matrix
As the sniper's bullet gently grazes the ear
Maybe he cut himself like an old wrestler
Blood & drama of a tv election
Sponsored by MKUltra

-124-
People walking in darkness
Because of the lack of light
Living in the shadow of Palestine
Where people die for no reason
For ownership of land
There is land for everyone
This is not our land
Meanwhile in america
Armed christian soldiers don't march anymore
They just shoot

-125-
The news lies
The Republican lies
The Democrat lies
The church lies
They lied when they told us it was a free country

They lied & called it democracy
They lied & said it was for the people
It's always good versus evil
Truth is in the streets where the people slave
On the plantation where the money circulates
Straight back to the master, whip cracker
Truth rarely gets heard anymore
With so many versions to filter through
History is buried treasure, that comes with a curse when opened
Evolution, transformation, purification who needs it
With the World they have built against it
Truth will set you free, seek it

-126-
Rockin' republicans to rain oppression on the poor
Trickling down like rain or scraps
Coming with strict religious oppression
Fear is at the controls
We don't understand our artists
So we're out there starving in the streets
No interest in beauty or creation, only destruction
Who will save us fatherless children
We must save ourselves or die trying

-127-
All over the World
People missing people
Waves of sorrow circulating
People tryin' to figure things out
With sorrow dragging them down
In spite of sorrow, in spite of ourselves
We dive into the unknown

Just the way we were meant to
So we may find ourselves

-128-
It's a chilling sound
Crowd chanting "Fight! Fight! Fight"
It's a bone chilling sound to me
Single thrust of language
A battle cry
Divisive, no it fights division
It's a single thrust into the soul of america
    a single thrust into the soul of the World
It is the cross and the gun, controlled spirituality
Imagine these people forever fighting everything
I have lost the urge to fight anything

-129-
Tonight I make words
Tonight I will set all of the crystals out
To charge under the full moon
Today is Buffie's birthday
I blow smoke in the wind

-130-
Reading Patti Smith from an Outlaw Bible
Brownie chasing flies across the floor
Darkness of a Florida thunderstorm
Thunder roars

-131-
What if I told you I talked to God today
She said she's sick of all the suffering

She's trying to do the right thing
She just spoke right into my head
I would guess God could do that

-132-
Father there is hate everywhere I look
Enough to scorch the Earth a million times over
You could just burn in all of that hate
I read that stored anger is the cause of liver cancer
All I know is I am trying to shed myself of it
Like an old snakeskin, that no longer fits me
I just want to be purified, free of heaviness

-133-
Poets grinding themselves to death
Just to keep the craft afloat
To keep it from sinking all the way in the gutter
How quickly they forgot
Bodies break like fallen soldiers
The ones that make art bigger than self
They get crushed by the weight of it
Of trying to hold it up all alone
No one notices

-134-
This is not my america
Fathers turn on children
For the choice of creation
Hangin' on by the skin of their teeth
Livin' this american dream
No money, but freedom money can't buy
This is not my america

-135-
Yesterday I did a reading
Yesterday I reignited a spark called Poetry
I now don't expect anything from it
I now feel so much freer
My old mentors in LA used to tell me
In all of their Poetic wisdom
A Poem is not born until it's read aloud
If that is the case as of yesterday
This Poem is alive

-136-
This insane World can't be real
As Buddha said a realm of suffering
The World on the tv does not seem authentic
Even the news feels like a cheap soap opera

-137-
Left and right making their pitch
For the soul of america
Souls been sucked out
America keeps following like soulless zombies
It follows whatever is shiny and cool
It follows all the latest trends
America gets easily distracted
Always listens when told
How to act and react
While being told it is free
Dying for anyone's sins besides our own

-138-
This is a time of purification

A time in life to purify
I seem to know the way by instinct
Like something I've done before
Meanwhile outside thunder roaring

-139-
There's a tropical storm on the way
Always a storm brewing
In the ocean of our fears
Just endless dark waters
Just endless possibilities
Something good could launch
From all of that darkness

-140-
Noise of a tropical storm
Muffled by noise of jazz
More climate change from the Atlantic
Wonder which time it hits you
& if you will survive it
The state wont even acknowledge it

-141-
They took freedom and put it in a cage
They took peace and injected it with rage
They took love and they split it up
They create just to self-destruct
They took fear and they made it god
They took God and they made her fear
They took the news and made it a lie
But there was plenty of stuff to buy
They took health and made it big business

They took cancer and fed it to us
They took the top of the pyramid
They put the boot down on us
They told us work would set us free

-142-
This is not my america
That turns an artist to an outcast
Maybe that's you, imprinted on me like a mark of shame
I guess it doesn't matter who's america it is anymore
We did not come here by choice
We were dropped here
We were given the illusion of free will
We were never told we create this reality
And we'd best create a better one

-143-
History has told us
That Merlin was a fatherless child
Quite literally the legend goes
Is this what we've become
Drifters searching the outer realms for ourselves
And when we find ourselves we come back different

-144-
I can't remember a lot about you
I can't remember a lot of anything
It's like a distant past life
And it's best I move away from it
I don't know which way forward is
As I journey further inside
It's the only way out of here

-145-
This is not my america
Lying nationalist dictators
Dick-tating to porn stars
america the conned
Leading by a landslide
Saved by god from an mkultra bullet
Just a troubled farm boy
Perfect shot at that distance
america has more guns than people
Got health issues
They can profit from
Got mental health issues
They can fear
Got sickness in the head
Kept so far away from what we are
Kept so far away from who we are
We are just slaves
And if you try to stay close to yourself
They will take that away from you
They will take your blood
They will take your father
You could not help that
You were just as they programed you to be
Though you tried to be different
In the end we turn out the same
Ground down by the system

-146-
After the rain
Air feels clean and new again
Jazz filling the air

The dog looks around for change
The World feels reborn

-147-
Jesus was the ultimate fatherless child
So let's all be martyrs and die for people's sins
It doesn't matter if you don't want to
It's for the greater good

-148-
Someday if I ever make it out of this prison
Fear standing guard to keep me from my potential
Fear standing guard to keep me in my cage
Projections like a movie playing in my head
It keeps spinning around like a big loop
Is that history repeating, or just DeJa'Vu

-149-
None of us know what death even is
It's fear of the unknown
Always fear, where we find our limits
I am not scared of death
I don't believe in it
I've seen some scary shit in this World
Some scary, slimy, traumatizing shit
Death, it doesn't exist
We can evolve or suffer
Suffering is so easy when you're numb to it
You don't even realize you're doing it
It's easy to get stuck in that place

-150-
I received a notification today
That a part of this Poem will be published
That will be the first part
The only part I've sent out so far
I read a part of it in Saint Augustine
With a Shaman Drum

-151-
Negative vibration trying to slip in
Trying to drag me back
To the land of cycles
I can't go back
I've come too far
& I've gone nowhere

-152-
They have taught us to fear death
At least not understand it
Truth is that we don't die
We evolve beyond the cycles
Or we are free to repeat them
Lately I feel a lot of negative energy creeping in
Trying to pull me back to the same old cycles
I'm too strong for it now

-153-
This is not my country
Children are abused,
            so confused
Politics is all bad news

Politian lying with a smile
While the poor man lies dying
How does one write
With all this dying going on

-154-
When they looked at their fears
They saw themselves looking back
Stuck in an endless cycle, trauma after trauma
They were scared of anything they didn't understand
& they didn't understand a lot
The great unknown

-155-
This is not my america
Genocidal butcher, arms dealer
Sacrificing lives for profits
It ain't me
I create, I do not destroy
No use in vicious modern societies
Not in these modern slave states
I was only born here
I have no shame
I drop no bomb
All I drop is truth in a World of lies
People fear what they don't understand

-156-
I have a steady wind at my back
Something keeping me fluid
Something showing me the way
Not that I want to go forward
But I sure don't want to go back

Release all of those things
Relive all of that trauma

-157-
There is little optimism
Cloud hanging over everything
Dusty Rhodes hard times
Here I am walking on instinct
Walking through a minefield
These days I try to keep a high vibration
Avoid lower level things

-158-
Politics has failed us
No one thinks about peace anymore
No one thinks in the noise of the television
It's like there were arms dealers running the government
It's like we have options, but peace is not one of them
Cycles keep repeating, we never learn beyond them
Succeed,
Become your own sovereign Poetic nation
You'll probably have to go out for supplies
Just play it cool, follow the rules
Don't let them find you

-159-
Baraka said death lives in the west
Where the sun goes to die
Clouds explode with light and color
Is that where you have gone
I am still here in hell, it gets hotter
No one else seems to notice beyond self
Motivated by a great fear of something

-160-

This is not my america
Fear is at the wheel
How does one survive
Like it was a disney ride
In some park you can't afford
I've been thinking about voting
How does one vote against the war
In a two party corporate war scam
Where they talk a good game
Say all the right things
They never answer to a lot
But who does

-161-

This is not my america
They told us we were free
Free to be what we want to be
Maybe a writer or Poet
Making such decisions one should be ready
For the onslaught of poverty
We as a society do not smile on creation
The same way destruction is the apple of our eye
If you don't believe me just turn on the tv
Let them tell you what you want to see
No one wants to be a Poet
They always die tragically
Sometimes at the hands of their governments

-162-

We never even knew america
We only knew what we were told

And only people that agree
I would agree this feels like an awkward silence
Right before the kill

-163-
I wonder at what point this Poem will end
At what point will I be cleansed of this shit
All of the negativity you have passed to me
That I never asked for
I've been spending too much time with myself
Obsessed with daily workouts and meditation
Sometimes God talks to me
If that's what she wants to be called
Who am I to argue
I could be wrong about this whole thing
She says we're all a piece of God

-164-
We have failed politics
Turnin' candidates to martyrs
Like anyone is gonna save us
Besides ourselves
Like anyone is so selfless
Not that one
Slick media jedi mind tricks

-165-
america it is Winter
Gill Scott's been forecasting it for decades
And the seasons they do change
If he could only see this shit
Frozen lifeless tundra coming around again

Like the constant cycles of life
Winter in america
Because the Summer is too fucking hot
But the breeze is cool this evening
The Jazz is always the same

-166-
This is all a tribute to you
Poem after Poem stacked high
It will never overshadow
The fact that you could not call
You would hang up if I called
Not even a phone call you were gone
How did we get here father
No, we can't go back anymore

-167-
Was it all real
Or was it just a simulation
I was told it was all unprocessed trauma
                it was all just a nightmare
That I woke up from
Straight into another nightmare

-168-
I feel like I've been in this prison all my life
Forever slavin' on the plantation
Workin' in the corporate fields for massa
Best hours of my life stuck in mindless repetition
Caught up in the repetition of an endless cycle
Passing over me like the seasons

-169-
Father all of my life I have lived in your shadow
As a child I was conditioned to run from your screams
Burying my head in the pillow
I'm trying to free myself from this prison I've built
Fear and trauma guard & warden
No one ever sees it, they just drag it around
Every day, collecting more, growing heavier
They keep pushing forward, dragging it behind them
Until they can't do it anymore

-170-
If none of it was real
Simulation after simulation
Looped together
Like cycles
I guess it's as real as we make it
I guess it's all we've got

-171-
Father I've been living in your shadow
A dark storm coming, electric
A storm of great rage
For years I've been running from myself
Now I've found peace right here
God herself has told me, this is what I'm here to do
The consequences of not doing it are quite severe
I had best get working for nothing
Loving this craft that never loves me back
But it's not about that
It's bigger than that, it's bigger than me, it's bigger than you
It flows through me like energy and is alive

-172-

We have failed art
Shooting for titles of self-importance
Poet Laureate of the beat down
We need to let art stand
Free of image or attachment
Only the images words paint
That's the only thing that matters

-173-

Father we have failed
By looking for a savior on the outside
They never told us
The Savior is on the inside
Inside of all of us
We are all the same
What I do to you
I do to myself
They knew it all along
Laughing at our ignorance
All the way to the bank

I no longer exist in that blissful ignorance
I no longer exist in that lower frequency
I have seen what our limits are
And they are equal to our fears
They are the same walls and limits they put there
They are the same walls you put there to survive
Outside those walls, forbidden knowledge
Hidden from sight, but in the range of influence
That same influence that whispers in your head
That voice that almost wasn't there

As tvs fill your brain with consumerism
                              processed foods to feed the cancer
Washed down with fluoride in the water supply

None of it matters anymore, it's too late
Said the shotgun to the head, wiser Poets have said before me
"She has come"

-174-
When we were children
We could see and hear other frequencies
As we go on with life
The spectrum narrows
Oh to truly see the World
Through the eyes of a child

-175-
The Poems they come
In the silence of my head
Like a voice
Leaving me to scribble it down
Leaving me to slow down the flow
Play with it, just because I can
It's the voices of the dead and living
All speaking through me
Spiritual state of creation

-176-
Father I have failed as an artist
Few actually see success anymore
I have successfully stirred up shit
Truth is I'm too honest for this World

Most writers are busy trying to eat each other
Or maybe suck each other off
What's the difference

-177-
An American protester was shot
By an israeli sniper
After the protest was over
She was just standing around
Then she wasn't
News forgot to report it
& a tree fell in the forest
And we can continue
To send them bullets and sniper rifles

-178-
If I had known what we were up against
I might not have made it this far
Maybe we're better off not knowing
All those things in the shadows
Yes angels are real
That could only mean
Demons are real too
That whisper inside your head
That draining of your energy field
That addiction to negative energy
With plenty to feed on
That name that must not be spoken aloud
Or you'll become a conspiracy theory
I don't give a fuck anymore
I'm telling the whole story
To save myself

-179-
We are not the best
As we would like to believe
The World is not ready for the word
Not true ones
Words with fleshy blood and real consequences
Wasting your life being a Poet
Intelligence went out in the World
No room for Poems with parts
And this one is beyond the hundreds

-180-
Know thyself is what they say
I know myself
I always have
Not as well as I do now
But a general direction
I've never been lost
Always found by the pen and page
And isn't it Poetic
But it's never paid the rent

-181-
All of my life we went to Saint Petersburg
We crossed the big bridge to get there
Your mother lived there
You bought the house from her when you retired
I knew how to get to the beach and the mall
I never knew Kerouac owned a house there
A house he lived in when he died
The city is a mystery to me

-182-
We are a divided conscience
Seeing only what we see
We are seeking collective conscience
We just don't know what it is
Can't conceive such a concept
Inside the mind, there are galaxies to explore
More than you'd ever know
With the mind numbing noise of the tv on
The mind cannot function
There is nothing there to find
Passing through trauma like mile markers
Wake up!

-183-
Life and it's betrayal
How low can we really go
You taught me a great lesson father
How easily I could be forgotten
Maybe I really did die back there
And I've just been walkin' around
A ghost all this time
I don't have much proof I'm not
There is this wound I am trying to heal
Right in the center of my gut
It takes a lot of time
Lately all I have is time
Rebuilding it all with a higher vibration
                          a higher consciousness
Trying to make something of this mess

-184-
Words fall into my head
From somewhere else entirely
Sun sets, dogs play
Cycle spinning like normal
Everyday program

-185-
I try not to fear much anymore
Watching darkness consume everything
How could I not fear
Most people wouldn't acknowledge it exist
So it just hangs around
I fear what is coming, growing stronger
It knows us all by name
It keeps us divided, wounded
Never realizing we are so much more

-186-
The mind is all we have left that's free
And that is questionable in this reality of illusion
These things we see that cannot be unseen
They might not even be real

-187-
Words come into my head from somewhere
Where, I don't know
I just wait to hear them
Then go with the flow
The weight of the World
Is on us all

I'm just trying to be Divine
Myself in a higher form

-188-
Pushing through life
Never processing anything
We are all just ghosts of ourselves
Slowly fading into nothing
Slowly fading from reality
Into the realm of spirit

-189-
The saxophone screams
Children scream from a backyard
The dog is screaming at the back door
Or screaming at the dogs down the street
Who are screaming
I used to see you in my nightmares father
You would just open your mouth
A huge deafening scream would come out

-190-
We all have P.T.S.D.
From the fucked up shit
That we've survived
Within this realm of suffering
I know you had your own wounds
I know you had your scars
I know you had your ghosts
No one walks through this hell
And comes out unscared
There is enough unprocessed trauma

To fill the World a million times over
We just walk like nothing happened

-191-
I'm homeless
Been homeless for years
I had a roof over my head
I can't even say where I have been
But I've been right here
I've traveled thousands of miles
And I've been right here

-192-
This is not my country
Where they shove chirstian nationalism
Down our throats like it was the only meal in town
Like there never was a choice in a fascist election
& the whole game has been fixed
It's down to the forth quarter
It's down with art
Nothing that creates anything
Mandatory bullet vending machines
To shut down spontaneous creation on sight
Concealed carry laws so we won't see it coming
It's down with light, darkness will rise
Be the light, be creation in the face of decline
Be the light, as dark as it may seem

-193-
Father I feel it is time
To let this go
I could extend it so it would have a million parts

It would still be the same, it would never solve anything
Look at it now, well over two hundred parts
Hardly worth the paper that it was printed on
Hardly scratched the surface of the World
Tomorrow I will write a new Poem
Not the same one I've been writing since February
Here we are on the last day of September
I feel it's time I must move on
And father, it's not like you're going to say anything
Just know that I love you and forgive you
I never wanted things to end this way
It's those things that are out of our control
Life can kill you, but not eat you
You always did say that

Over the years **Michael D. Grover** has become a legendary
underground Poet. Back in the early 2000s he ran Covert Press and
worked with many of the giants of underground Poetry. Over the
years Michael has been published in countless publications all over
the World, and published over fifteen books of Poetry. Michael
spent over ten years as head Poetry editor of the literary zine *Red
Fez*. Michael has published two novels. Michael currently lives in
Florida, dealing with cancer, with his dog where he meditates every
day.

MORE ROADSIDE PRESS TITLES

MORE ROADSIDE PRESS TITLES

MORE ROADSIDE PRESS TITLES

Current Disasters
Jen McConnell

Better Than The Best American Poetry
Dave Newman

Little Graveyards
Aleathia Drehmer

The Screw City Poems
Richard Vargas

*and all of us drinking the blood
of our enemies*
John Sweet

This Is Where We Are
Nicholas Claro

*Perseverance: The Making of a
Musician*
Steven Grey

with her hair on fire
Christy Prahl